Cooking Up a story

by **Mary Medlicott**

Illustrated by Martha Hardy

Cooking Up a Story

ISBN 1 905019 00 9

Written by Mary Medlicott

Illustrations by Martha Hardy

Editing and design by Phill Featherstone

© Featherstone Education Ltd, 2004
Text © Mary Medlicott, 2004
Illustrations © Martha Hardy, 2004

All rights reserved.

First published in the UK, October 2004

Published in the United Kingdom by
Featherstone Education Ltd
44-46 High Street
Husbands Bosworth
Leicestershire
LE17 6LP

Printed in the UK on paper produced in the European Union from managed, sustainable forests

Welcome to the Storytime Kitchen

Storytime is too important to be neglected or treated as just another chore. It can contribute vitally to young children's lives, giving them what they need to grow up healthy - food for the imagination, nourishment for the emotions and a chance to make sense of the world in which we live.

***Cooking Up a Story** offers a fresh approach to storytime. The focus is on oral storytelling, an activity that goes back many centuries to something very old and precious in human culture. At its heart lies an engagement between storyteller and audience that allows plenty of space for imaginative listening and lots of room for participation. Without in any way excluding books from storytime, it suggests a renewed emphasis on storytelling without the book. All of the stories have been specially prepared for this book. Some of them are my own, original stories; others are re-workings of traditional plots, ideas and themes. Where I've used stories by other people, the author or source is given. All of them have been tried many times with children.*

*Within **Cooking Up a Story**, you will find a wide choice of individual dishes for putting together your storytime menus. The selection includes stories for telling without a book as well as chants, rhymes and games for the imagination - all arranged in such a way as to allow you to combine the dishes differently for different occasions. There are also hints on serving up all these items in new and lively ways. I hope the selection will provide you with plenty of fresh ideas and support you in looking again at the unique role that stories and storytime can play in Early Years education.*

***Cooking Up a Story** arose from a major early years storytelling project in the London Borough of Enfield, a hugely diverse area both ethnically and economically. The project involved a very large number of nursery classes and playgroups, and demonstrated how much enjoyment and benefit storytime can bring to adults and children alike.*

Stories and storytelling are at the heart of what we are and can be as human beings. Everyone enjoys a good story. I hope you enjoy my stories, and this book.

Happy Cooking!

Mary Medlicott
Storyteller

Menu

All rhymes, adaptations and stories are by Mary Medlicott, unless attributed otherwise

Aperitif

Your storytime diet; some general principles for planning storytime

Allow plenty of time for your storytime. It's not pleasant for storyteller or audience to feel rushed, and hurrying will spoil your stories. Good timing builds interest and tension.

Create a well-balanced storytime by mixing and matching rhymes, games and stories.

Try telling a story without relying on a book. You can always include a picture book in your session if you need some illustrations.

Repeat your stories on several successive occasions to enable children to get to know them. Familiarity will increase their enjoyment.

Try bringing storytime forward so that it happens earlier in your morning or afternoon session, when the children are fresh and their minds are lively. You can always have an end-of-session story or rhymetime as well.

Appetisers

Joining-in chants and imagination games for getting children involved

'Ssh! Listen!' – a joining-in chant

Start by tapping your knees gently in a rhythmical way. Tap until you're sure you have the attention of all the children. Then say these words in time with the tapping:

> **It's storytime, it's storytime!**
> **Ssh! Listen!**
> **What's going on?**

After a pause, repeat the chant, looking around at the children. When you say "Ssh!" put your finger to your lips. When you say "Listen!" cup your hand around your ear.

Extra interest can be added by introducing one or two sound-making instruments - a tambourine, a drum, a bell, a rainstick. Set the instruments out in front of you before you start, or have them ready in a bag beside you. After getting everyone going with the chant, pick up one of the instruments ("Listen!") and demonstrate its sound.

If you think it's appropriate, give the children a chance to talk about the sound they've heard before you return to the chant.

Or you could bring along an interesting object, maybe something that relates to the story you're planning to tell:

> **What's going on?**
> **What's this in my bag?**
> **What's this object doing here?**

Variations

Here's another example of a joining-in chant:

> **Wiggle your fingers, wiggle your toes**
> **We might have a story that nobody knows.**
> **Tell it fast or tell it slow.**
> **Listen to the story, here we go.**

You could have a go at making up a joining-in chant of your own.

'What's it for?' – an imagination game

Tap your knees and click your fingers as you start the first line of this rhyme. As you say line two, tap your knees and open your hands in an inquiring gesture.

Here's a very fine piece of cloth.
But what's it for? What's it for?

Now ask the children if anyone has an idea of what the cloth could be for. Maybe there's a boy in your grou called, let's call him Abdul, who suggests it could be used for a cloak. You can then invite Abdul to come out to the front and show how he would use the cloth as a cloak. You might comment, "That's a good idea, Abdul. Look at Abdul wearing his cloak." Then continue:

So Abdul says it's for a cloak.
But could it be for anything else?
Let's see!
Here's a very fine piece of cloth.
But what's it for? What's it for?

Maybe someone called Tracey says, "A bed-cover!" Tracey, too, can come out to the front and demonstrate her idea. Again, you might comment, "That's a good idea, Tracey. Look at Tracey pulling up her bed-cover. Goodnight Tracey!" Then continue:

So Abdul says it's for a cloak.
Tracey says it's for a bed-cover.
But could it be for anything else?
Let's see!

... and so on.

Allow plenty of time for this activity. Lots of children will want to have a go -

which is great.

Variations

If you've got a piece of cloth that could itself be a prop for a story, you could bring the game to an end like this:

> And I've got an idea as well.
> Perhaps the cloth is for telling a story! Shall I get ready to tell you the story?

The game is adaptable in other ways too. Instead of using a cloth try a piece of string.

> Here's a nice long piece of string.
> But what could it be for? What could it be for?

Or what about a woolly hat?

> Here's a nice warm woolly hat.
> But where could you go in this hat, do you think?
> Where could you go in this hat?
> To school? To a football match? Out to play?

'The Sea is Deep' – an imagination game

Introduce the rhyme below, with appropriate gestures.

> The sea is deep,
> The sea is wide.
> The sea's got lots of things inside.
> It's got …? .... fishes!

Show an action to represent fishes. Then repeat the rhyme, encouraging everyone to join in.

> And I wonder what else the sea has got inside it?
> The sea is deep,
> The sea is wide.
> The sea's got lots of things inside.
> It's got fishes and …? ....a crab!

Ask the person who has suggested a crab for an action to represent it. Or suggest one yourself. Again, encourage everyone to echo the gesture. Then continue:

> And I wonder what else is in the sea?
> The sea is deep,
> The sea is wide.
> The sea's got lots of things inside.
> It's got fishes and a crab ... and...? .... seaweed!

Once more, ask for a gesture, encourage everyone to join in and continue until you feel it's time to stop.

Hints on telling

- *Movements of your hands can suggest the depth and width of the sea, also that your audience is being invited to say what the sea may have inside it. Raised eyebrows and an expectant look on your face help them know that it's now their turn to contribute.*
- *It's vital to come up with an action or gesture for each of the sea's contents as it gets added to the game. This helps everyone to remember the sequence and build it up.*
- *Children usually volunteer an appropriate action or gesture to go with the idea that has been given. If they don't, you may have to help out.*
- *Children appreciate it very much if you mirror the particular way they make their gesture.*
- *It is often helpful to find a sound effect for an item as well as a gesture.*

Variations

1. *Try setting the game in a forest instead of the sea.*

> The forest is deep and the forest is wide.
> The forest's got lots of things inside.
> It's got...? .... foxes!
> And I wonder what else!

2. *Or what about a castle?*

> Let's go round the castle. What can we see?
> It's big and old.
> Just follow me!
> Look here!
> What's this? ... treasure?
> And I wonder what else we'll see!

'Magic Pot' – an imagination game

In this game everyone has a little magic pot. Cup your hands together to suggest the pot. Your upper hand is the lid of the pot. You can move it aside to peer into the pot and see what's hidden inside.

> **Here's a little magic pot!**
> **Look inside and see what you've got!**

After telling everyone what you think is inside your pot, suggest that they do the same. Formalise the game by repeating the rhyme after each child has had a go.

> **Here's a little magic pot!**
> **Look inside and see what you've got!**

Allow time for each child to have a turn if they want to.

Variations

Other versions of this game exist with slightly different wordings of the rhyme. This is a simplified version. You can alter it as you wish.

1. *Names of children can be added. For example:*
   > **Amy's got a magic pot!**
   > **Look inside, Amy, and see what you've got!**

2. *Particular themes can be added on different occasions. Specifying a theme can help stimulate the children to come up with ideas. For instance, you could suggest that each person finds a different animal in their magic pot. Or you could think of different sorts of food. Or find different places in the pot such as the beach, the forest or a shop. Or you could find different characters from nursery rhymes or picture books.*

Action rhymes, stories and chants to mix and match with your main stories

'Five Little Monkeys' – a counting rhyme

Five little monkeys jumping on the bed,
One fell off and bumped his head.
Mummy called the doctor
And the doctor said:
"No more monkeys jumping on the bed."

Four little monkeys jumping on the bed

until:

No little monkeys jumping on the bed!

Hints on telling

- *Hold up the appropriate number of fingers at the beginning of the rhyme.*
- *Or have five children come out front to 'be' the monkeys.*
- *Touch your head dramatically to suggest the bump on the head.*
- *Wag your finger reprovingly when the doctor speaks.*

'Little Mouse' – a nursery rhyme

A little mouse lived in a hole,
Deep down inside the hole.
All was quiet as quiet can be…
When OUT popped the mouse and frightened me.

Hints on telling

- *Make a loose fist of your left hand, and point down inside it to suggest the mouse's hole.*
- *Put your finger to your lips and hush your voice for line three.*
- *Bring your right forefinger quickly up through your fist to show the mouse popping out.*

'Where are the Bees?' – a traditional finger rhyme

Here is the beehive
But where are the bees?
Far inside where nobody sees.
Open the hive
And out they come
One, two, three, four, five.

Hints on telling

- *Make your hand into a fist to represent the beehive.*
- *Point into your fist when you ask where the bees are.*
- *Unfold your fingers one by one to suggest the bees flying out.*

Variations

The last line of the rhyme is sometimes as follows:

bzz... bzz... bzz... bzz... bzz

'Where's the Sun?' – a traditional English rhyme

What's in there?
Gold and money
Where's my share?
Mousie ran away with it
Where's the mousie?
In her housie
Where's her housie?
In the wood
Where's the wood?
Fire burned it
Where's the fire?
Water put it out
Where's the water?
Brown bull drank it
Where's the brown bull?
Back o' Burnie's hill
Where's Burnie's hill?
All covered in snow
Where's the snow?
Sun melted it
Where's the sun?
HIGH, HIGH, UP IN THE SKY

Hints on telling

Gestures help young children to understand and enjoy this rhyme.

- *For the first line, make your hand into a fist and point into your fist.*

- *For the second line, rub your finger on your palm to suggest gold and money.*

- *Open your hands in an enquiring gesture for "Where's my share?" and each subsequent question.*

- *Make a skittering side-to-side movement with one hand for the mousie.*

- *Shape your hands into a house-shape for mousie's house.*

- *Raise up your hands while fluttering your fingers to make flames for the fire; lower them, again with fingers fluttering, to suggest rain water coming down.*

- *Lean forward and pretend to gulp water when you get to the brown bull.*

- *Make a smoothing gesture with your hands to suggest the snow.*

- *Raise your hands in a circular gesture for the sun.*

- *Point upwards to indicate where the sun is.*

It is also helpful if you change the direction of your gaze between questions and answers - for instance, leftwards for questions, rightwards for answers.

Make variations in the tone of your voice, not only to emphasise the difference between questions and answers but also to suggest the changing atmosphere, for instance the quiet of the snow-covered landscape.

Cooking Up a Story

'Mrs Wiggle and Mrs Waggle' – a traditional action-story

Action

In this action story, your two thumbs represent Mrs Wiggle and Mrs Waggle and your hands become their houses. Tuck down your thumb to show them going into their house. Close your hand around your thumb when they close their door.

Story summary

One day, Mrs Wiggle goes to see Mrs Waggle, but she's not at home. The next day, Mrs Waggle goes to see Mrs Wiggle and *she's* not at home. The day after that, the two women both set out to see each other. They meet in the middle!

Full story

Introduce the characters.

Here's Mrs Wiggle. She's got a house. Look, she's opening the door, she's going inside. Now she's closing the door.

Mrs Wiggle has got a friend, Mrs Waggle. Mrs Waggle lives in her own house. Look, she's opening the door and going inside. Now she's closing the door.

Part one of the action

One morning, Mrs Wiggle woke up early. She decided to go to see her friend. She got ready, opened the door, went out of the house and closed the door. Then she set off. Up the hill and down the hill, up the hill and down the hill, up the hill and down the hill, until she came to her friend's house.

When she got to Mrs Waggle's, Mrs Wiggle knocked on the door. Knock, knock. No reply.

She knocked again. No reply. She called through the letter-box. "Mrs Waggle... Mrs Waggle..." No reply. So Mrs Wiggle went home, down the hill, until she got to her house.

She opened the door, went inside, closed the door and had a nice cup of tea.

Part two of the action

The next day, Mrs Waggle woke up in the morning and decided to go and see her friend.

(Repeat the journey that Mrs Wiggle made, including having to go home.)

Part three of the action

The day after that, Mrs Wiggle and Mrs Waggle both woke up at the same time and both decided to go and see their friend.

(Repeat all the actions as above until the two of them meet on the last hill.)

"Hello, hello. Fancy seeing you here. I was just coming to see you." Kiss, kiss, hug, hug.

Then Mrs Wiggle and Mrs Waggle had a nice long chat until it was time for them to go back home. "Bye, Bye. See you later."

So off they went, down the hill and up the hill and down the hill, until they both got home. Then they each went inside and had a nice cup of tea. And both of them said the very same thing: "Isn't it nice to have a friend?"

Hints on telling

- *Use a little beeping sound to punctuate some of the actions - opening the door, going inside, closing the door. This can amuse the children and help them join in.*
- *Make extravagant gestures, such as for waking up or drinking a cup of tea. This also helps the story to be amusing.*
- *Allow the children to remind you of what's about to happen as they pick up the pattern of the story.*
- *You can elaborate greatly on the story while you tell it. For instance, you could add your own explanations of why Mrs Wiggle and Mrs Waggle didn't open their door. Maybe they were asleep? Maybe they had already gone out?*
- *Or you could extend the storytelling by making up a good gossipy conversation when Mrs Wiggle and Mrs Waggle meet on the hill.*

Variations

1. *Instead of Mrs Wiggle and Mrs Waggle, your story could be about two men, Mr Wiggle and Mr Waggle.*

2. *When the characters meet on the hill, you could change the story by getting them to play a game; for example, hide-and-seek. As each character goes off to hide, conceal your fist behind your back.*

3. *Or, after the two characters meet on the hill, divert them to another venue, such as a cafe, a clothes shop, a park or the swimming pool. Use your fingers and thumbs to suggest where they go and what they do.*

'Going on a Bear-Hunt' – an action-chant

Story summary

In this story, we go out to find a bear and on the way overcome various obstacles. When we finally see the bear, we run away because we think the bear is chasing us. We get home just in time!

Full version

We're going on a bear hunt, a bear hunt, a bear hunt...
Oh what a lovely day!
I'm not scared, I'm not scared...

Oh look... tall, thick grass!
We can't go over it, we can't go under it.
We'll have to go through it.
Get ready to make a path through the grass!
SWISH! SWISH! SWISH!
Everybody through?

We're going on a bear hunt, a bear hunt, a bear hunt...
Oh what a lovely day!
I'm not scared, I'm not scared...

Oh look... squelchy brown mud!
We can't go over it, we can't go under it.
We'll have to go through it.
Get your boots on!
SHLUCK! SHLUCK! SHLUCK!
Everybody through?

We're going on a bear hunt, a bear hunt, a bear hunt...
Oh what a lovely day!
I'm not scared, I'm not scared...

Oh look ... a fast rushing river!
We can't go over it, we can't go under it.
We'll have to go through it.
Get ready to swim!
SPLASH! SPLASH! SPLASH!
Everybody through?

We're going on a bear hunt, a bear hunt, a bear hunt...
Oh what a lovely day!
I'm not scared, I'm not scared...

Oh look... a deep, dark cave!
We can't go over it, we can't go under it.
We'll have to go inside it.
Get ready to tiptoe inside!
SHH! SHH! SHH!

Everybody see him?
Two big brown eyes, two big furry ears, a big wet nose...
It's a bear! Run!!

Back through the river... the mud... the grass...
Back home. Open the door. Up the stairs. Into bed. Hide...
Here's Mum!
"Mum! Guess where I've been!
I've been on a bear hunt and seen a bear. And I wasn't a bit scared."

Were YOU?

Hints on telling

- *Before starting, it's a good idea to explain that you are NOT going on a bear hunt to kill a bear or hurt a bear. You are going to SEE a bear.*
- *Be purposeful and definite. Get your voice into a sing-song mood. Tap your knees in rhythm: "We're going on a BEAR-hunt, a BEAR-hunt, a BEAR-hunt."*
- *As you spot an obstacle - grass, mud, a river - fix your eyes on an imaginary spot somewhere in front of you and get some drama into your voice: "OH NO!"*
- *Use your body. Swing your arms to shove the grasses aside. Lift your legs to pull them through the mud. Swim vigorously through the river.*
- *When you get to the cave, change your voice to a quiet, hushed voice. If you wish, add new details such as "Ugh! cobwebs!" as you enter the cave.*
- *When you see the bear, make spectacle eyes. Put your hands to your head to show his ears. Tap your nose when you mention his nose.*

- *Imitate running as you start running away. From this point on, all actions are speeded up and occur in quick motion.*
- *During the dialogue with mum, pretend to be talking as a child.*

Variations

1. *Create fresh obstacles such as a frozen lake as the children become familiar with the pattern of the story.*
2. *Or turn the last part of the story into a role play, for example using cloths over an easel to make a cave where the bear can hide. Take different groups of children to visit the bear. Give children turns at being the bear, practising growling and raising their claws.*
3. *Or turn the whole thing into an action play, physically leading children on the bear hunt. First arrange the classroom, hall or an outside space into appropriate areas. Then all take part in the journey, moving around in a long line.*
4. *Or use the pattern of the story to create a whole new version such as 'Going to See Father Christmas' (coming next).*

'Going to See Father Christmas' – an original action story

We're going to see Father Christmas, Christmas, Christmas.
Oh what a chilly day!
I'm not scared! I'm not scared!
Oh look... it's a busy supermarket with everyone doing their Christmas shopping!
We can't get over it, we can't get under it,
We'll have to push through it.
'SCUSE ME!... 'SCUSE ME!... 'SCUSE ME!...

Repeat the basic rhyme until:

Oh look... a frozen lake!
We can't get over it, we can't get under it,
We'll have to slide across it.
SWISH!... SWISH!... SWISH!...

Repeat, adding a wall of ice. Then:

Shh! Can you hear the sound of reindeer bells?
TING!... TING!... TING!...
Can you see a lighted window?
It's Father Christmas's House.
Let's tiptoe over and look in.

Shh! There's Father Christmas's reindeers.
Shh! There's Father Christmas wrapping presents.

Look, he's wrapping a present for me.
Quick! We'll have to get home before he reaches our house.

Then run home, going back through the actions.

Run!
Back through the wall of ice.
Over the frozen lake.
Through the supermarket... only a few people left.
Quick! Into the house. Up the stairs. Jump into bed.

Oh, here's mum!
"Mum, we've been to see Father Christmas... and he's got a Christmas present for me!"

Hints on telling

* *Emphasise the wintry atmosphere with lots of shivering, clutching arms, etc.*
* *You can introduce the song 'Jingle Bells, Jingle Bells' when you come across the reindeer.*

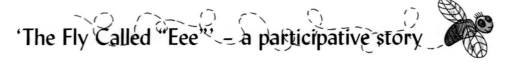

'The Fly Called "Eee" – a participative story

(adapted from a Sri Lankan tale)

Story summary

One day, the fly forgets his name - "Eee". He goes to look for some creatures who may be able to remind him what he is called. But the creatures he finds speak only their own languages. At last he finds someone who can help him. In the traditional Sri Lankan version, this creature was a horse. The neigh of the horse sounds like "Eee". In this version it's a child who helps by remembering the name.

Simple version

In the faraway country of Sri Lanka, the fly has got a special name: "Eee" (to rhyme with bee).

But one day, something awful happened. The fly called "Eee" forgot his name. (What a thing to do! You wouldn't do that, would you?) This is how it came about.

When "Eee" woke up in the morning, he tried to remember his name but however hard he tried, he couldn't do it. He felt so upset and worried that he decided to go out of his house and look for someone who might help him.

None of the creatures he met could help him. They only said their own sounds.

Then at last he met some children.

(You can pretend the fly has come into your own nursery or school if you like).

He asked them his name and they all said: "Eee!"

Hints on telling

- *This story provides a good chance to practise your animal noises and learn some new ones from your audience. When I first heard it, it was told in a very simple style. You can follow that example, putting the story into your own words.*
- *Or you can make the story highly participative, inviting individual children to come out and 'perform' for the others. After the fly has met a dog and a cat, ask the children if they can think of any other animals that could be in the story and if they can make their noises.*
- *When hands go up, invite a child to come out to the front to be in the story. Pick up the idea by pretending to be the fly asking the 'animal' if he or she knows your name: "Can you possibly tell me my name?" After the child has made the animal-noise, you could sound a bit sad that it's not your name but then, as the storyteller, cheerfully thank the child for taking part in the story and give the child a clap. Even very shy children often take the chance to participate in this story. Many rise to the occasion with enormous humour.*
- *Or you can tell the story in my rap version below.*

Rap version of 'The Fly Called "Eee"'

Once upon a time
There was a fly called "Eee".
Who's he?
"That's me!" said the fly called "Eee".

Well one sunny day, that fly he went to bed
And he woke up in the morning
With a pain in his head.
So he went to the doctor
And the doctor said, "Name?
Please will you tell me your name."

The fly said, "SURE!
'Course I'll tell you my name.
My name is.........Oh! I've forgotten my name!
I've gone and forgotten my name!
Now nothing will ever be the same...
Unless there's someone who can tell me my name."

So the fly got up and flew down the road,
Looking for a friend.

Down the road he met the dog.
"Scuse me, Dog," said the fly.
"Can you possibly tell me my name?"
The dog said, "WOOF! WOOF! WOOF! WOOF!"
(He could only speak dog language.)

But the fly said, "No, that's not MY name.
That's definitely not my name.
Now nothing will ever be the same if I can't remember my name."

So the fly got up and flew on down the road,
Looking for a friend.
Down the road he met the cat....
"Scuse me, Cat," said the Fly. "Can you please tell me my name?"
The Cat replied, "MEEAOW..."

Repeat as above as the fly meets lots of different animals, according to the children's suggestions. The children can join in by making appropriate sounds, and if you wish they can come out to the front to be the particular animal.

Finally, of course, the fly must meet someone who can tell him his name. Could it be a child? The children in your group? Whoever it is, make sure the fly sounds very, very pleased when you and the children tell him that his name is "Eee".

"Yes! Yes!" said the fly,
"That is my name. That definitely is my name.
Now everything can be the same
Because you've remembered my name.
Thank you."
And that is the end of my game.

Hints on telling

- *Tap your knees and click your fingers in rhythm with the words of the rhyme ...tap ...click...; tap... click... tap... click... tap... Don't worry if you're no good at clicking. Many of your audience won't be able to do it either. Tapping your knees will do instead. But it's important to make the action feel cheerful and fun. Joining in with the rhythm helps children focus and participate.*

Stories for telling without the book, plus suggestions for follow-up activities

Sun Frog and Moon Frog

(retold from a story by Penny Bernand of Pop-Up Theatre)

Story summary

Two frogs are visited by a strange bird who tells them they are in danger and offers to help them. They refuse. She returns, they refuse again. The third time she comes back, they are in real danger and ask for her help. After taking them to a safe place, she tells them how they can remember her in future.

Full version

Once upon a time, there were two frogs, Moon Frog and Sun Frog. They lived in a pond with a rock for jumping and they had a lovely time doing nothing but jumping, staring, blinking, winking and licking the air for flies.

One day they had a visitor: the tikki-tikki bird, with her beautiful tail of many-coloured feathers.

The tikki-tikki bird said she wanted to help them. Terrible rains were coming; their pond would turn into a rushing river and they would not be safe even though they were used to living in water. She said she could help them find a new pond to move to. But Moon Frog and Sun Frog ignored her. "Rubbish!" said Sun Frog. "Silly!" said Moon Frog.

Soon the storm began. In the midst of the rain, the tikki-tikki bird returned with her beautiful tail of many-coloured feathers. Once again, Sun Frog and Moon Frog didn't want to listen.

But after a while, the rain became too heavy even for Sun Frog and Moon Frog. At last they found a tree to climb. But by the time they reached the top, there was water all round them. Where were they going to go? What were they going to do? They wished they had listened to the tikki-tikki bird.

Suddenly, the tikki-tikki bird came back. The two frogs asked her to help them. She said she was still willing to take them somewhere safe. This time the two frogs listened. They jumped on her back and she flew through the sky until she came to a place where it was no longer raining. There the frogs saw a different pond where the water was calm. When the tikki-tikki bird flew down, they jumped in the water and started doing what they liked best - jumping, staring, blinking, winking and licking the air for flies.

When the tikki-tikki bird said goodbye, she told them that in future, when there was sun after rain, if they looked up in the sky, they might see her there and remember that she was their friend. And that is what they did. Every time it finished raining, they looked up in the sky and whenever they saw the rainbow with all its lovely colours, they remembered the tikki-tikki bird and her beautiful tail of many-coloured feathers.

Hints on telling

- *Actions are important to this story.*
  Make spectacle eyes when introducing the frogs. Use your elbows to create the sense of two frogs jumping. Spectacle eyes give the sense of the two frogs staring. Take time over winking and blinking. Use your tongue to suggest the two frogs licking the air for flies. Cross your hands and flap them in the air, lowering and raising them to suggest the flight of the tikki-tikki bird.
- *There's also plenty of opportunity for sound effects.*
  Children like frog noises. Try sinking your voice into your stomach and sucking in your breath as you speak. Just lowering your voice will do. The sounds of the storm can be created by the whole group. For lightning, shoot hands up into the air with a sharp crack of your voice. For thunder, start with hands high up in a fist, then hammering down onto your knees. For rain, start with clicking fingers, then hands brushed together, then fists on knees and finally feet hammering on the floor. The sound of the tikki-tikki bird is as her name suggests: tikki... tikki...
- *Props add to the interest of the story.*
  A multi-coloured cloth can represent the tikki-tikki bird's tail. A puppet frog is also a good idea, not to take part in the story but to introduce the characters.

Follow-up activities

Children really enjoy making pictures of this story. Ask them to choose their favourite part of the story and make a picture of that.

'Rabbit's Lucky Escape' – a folk-tale from East Africa

Story summary

Rabbit goes by mistake into Lion's den. When Lion comes back, she has to think quickly to get herself out of trouble. She pretends to be King of the Lions, taking a rest in the den. When Lion fetches other friends, Elephant, Snake, etc., Rabbit pretends to be King of the Elephants, King of the Snakes, etc. Finally, when the animals get too suspicious and threaten to come into the den, she says she is King of All the Animals and they must close their eyes and bow down when she comes out because she is too important for them to see her. Thus Rabbit makes her escape.

Full version

One day Rabbit goes into Lion's den by mistake. She falls asleep. But when Lion comes home, he stops at the entrance. He knows there's someone inside.

"Who's in my den?" he roars. "Come out, or I, Lion, am coming in."

Rabbit wakes up. She is frightened. But she gets a good idea. She pretends to be King of the Lions.

"I'm the King of the Lions," she says in her loudest voice. "I'm having a rest in your den. You'll have to wait."

Lion is not sure what to do. He goes and fetches Elephant. Elephant trumpets, "Who's in my friend Lion's den? Come out or I, Elephant, am coming in."

Rabbit is frightened again. But now she pretends to be the King of the Elephants.

"I'm the King of the Elephants. I'm having a rest in Lion's den. You'll have to wait."

Lion and Elephant are not convinced. Who is really in Lion's den? Is someone just pretending to be a King? They go and fetch Snake. Snake hisses loudly, "Who's in my friend Lion's den? Come out or I, Snake, am coming in."

Rabbit pretends to be King of the Snakes. But the animals can't believe that so many Kings are inside Lion's den. They say, "Come out of Lion's den or we're all coming in."

Now Rabbit is really, really frightened - until she gets the best idea of all. She pretends to be King of ALL the Animals.

"Don't you understand?" she shouts in her loudest, grandest voice. "I'm King of ALL the Animals. And now I've had my rest, I'm ready to come out of this den. But first you must bow down and close your eyes, for I'm too important for you to see me."

The animals bow down and close their eyes and Rabbit hops out of the den. Only Lion peeks out of the corner of his eye. And when he sees who it is, he goes chasing after. But by then, Rabbit has reached home and is safe inside.

Hints on telling

- *To set the scene for this story, take a bit of time introducing the two main characters. For Rabbit, make long ears, twitch your nose and show her hoppity, skippety way of moving. For Lion, suggest how hungry he is by rubbing your hands over your stomach and show him walking about with a loping, greedy sort of gait. Also introduce the places where the two main characters live. Rabbit has a small little house. Lion has a big shadowy den. Draw them in the air.*
- *Take the many opportunities for children to join in with what the characters say. Use a big loud voice when Lion and his friends are talking. Use a small high frightened voice when Rabbit is talking to herself about what she is going to do. Use a big confident voice when Rabbit is talking to the animals.*
- *Show the emotions of the story. Play-act being very angry when Lion and his friends get cross: wave your fists in the air or hammer your fists on your knees. Play-act at being very frightened when Rabbit hears Lion and his friends outside the den: tap your hand against your chest to give the impression of extreme nervousness.*
- *Invite ideas from the children. Ask the children to suggest which animals Lion went to fetch. Summon up the character of these animals with various gestures or noises. For example, swing an arm in front of your head to suggest Elephant's trunk. Raise your hands to your ears to indicate his large flappy ears. Use your arm and hissing sounds to suggest Snake.*

Follow-up activities

1. *Invite the children to draw pictures of the story. A series of pictures on a foldout or zig-zag book is effective.*
2. *Encourage role-play. In your building-blocks area, suggest the children create Rabbit's house and Lion's den. Or whisper the idea that the climbing frame in your outside play area might become Lion's den.*

'The Naughty Little Mouse' – a traditional tale

Story summary

A mouse goes out and persuades three shopkeepers into:
1. Giving her some cloth
2. Making her a hat
3. Decorating the hat
Then the mouse manages to persuade the queen into letting her sit on the throne for a day. When she gets home, she's got a good story to tell - and a pretty hat!

Full version

There was once a little mouse who one day went out for a walk. As she went along she sang her song: "La la, la la, la la, la la." Soon the mouse came to a shop. It was a shop that sold cloth. The mouse went into the shop.

"Give me a piece of your cloth," she said to the man inside.

"No," said the man, "You're just a mouse."

"Give me a piece of your cloth," said the mouse, "or I'll come back here tonight with all of my friends and we'll eat all the cloth in your shop."

"O-o-h!" said the man. "Go away. You're a very naughty little mouse."

Then the mouse remembered a word she could use. "Oh P-L-E-A-S-E-?" she said.

"That's better," said the man. "Now you've said 'please', I'll give you a piece of cloth. But only a small piece."

The man went into the back of the shop where he kept his scissors. He cut a small piece of cloth. When he came back, he gave it to the mouse. She was very pleased. She took the cloth and went out of the shop, singing her song as she went down the road: "La la, la la, la la, la la."

Then she came to another shop. It was a shop that made hats. The mouse went inside. "Make me a hat from my piece of cloth," she said to the lady inside.

"No," said the lady, looking up from her sewing. "You're only a mouse. Get out of my shop."

"Make me a hat from my piece of cloth," said the mouse, "or I'll come back here with my friends tonight and we'll eat holes in all the hats in your shop."

"T-s-h!" said the lady. "You are a very NAUGHTY little mouse."

"Oh P-L-E-A-S-E?" said the little mouse.

"Very well then," said the lady. "You did say 'please'. So I'll make you a hat. But just a plain one."

The lady took the cloth from the little mouse and sewed it into a hat. When she brought it out, the little mouse was very pleased. She put it on and went out of the shop, singing her song as she went down the road: "La la, la la, la la, la la."

Down the road, the naughty little mouse came to another shop that sold pretty things for decorating clothes: buttons and braids and silk flowers and sequins. The mouse went inside.

"Sew some pretty things onto my hat," she said to the man inside.

"No," said the man. "You're just a mouse. Get out of my shop."

"Sew some pretty things onto my hat," said the little mouse, "or I'll come back here with my friends tonight and we'll eat up all the stuff in your shop."

"Off with you!" said the man. "You're a very naughty little mouse."

"Oh P-L-E-A-S-E?" said the little mouse.

"Very well then," said the man. "You did say 'please'. So I'll sew some pretty things onto your hat. But just a few!"

The man took the hat to the back of the shop and decorated it. When he brought it back, it looked very pretty and the little mouse was very pleased. She put it on and went out of the shop and as she went she sang her song: "La la, la la, la la, la la."

Soon she came to the gates of the palace where the queen lived. The mouse ran inside and looked around until she came to the throne where the queen was sitting. The throne was covered with red velvet cushions.

"Let me sit on your throne," said the mouse.

"No," laughed the queen. "You're only a mouse."

"If you don't let me sit on your throne," said the mouse, "I'll come back here with all my friends tonight, and we'll eat your red velvet cushions."

"Dear me," said the queen. "You're a very naughty little mouse."

"Oh P-L-E-A-S-E?" said the naughty little mouse.

"Very well then," said the queen. "You did say please. You can sit on my throne. But only for one day!"

The queen got up and went out of the throne room. The naughty little mouse ran up the side of the throne and sat on the red velvet cushions. She felt so proud as she looked around. But at the end of the day, she remembered her house and wanted to go home. She ran down the throne, out of the palace and along the road and as she went she sang her song: "La la, la la, la la, la la."

Cooking Up a Story

When the mouse got home, she was so tired she went straight to bed. But she didn't take her hat off. She slept in it all night long and in the morning when she woke, she went out of the house to go and find her friends. And when she found them, she told them everything that had happened the day before. She told them exactly the story I've just told you now.

Hints on telling

- *Use different tones in your voice to good effect. Use your voice to convey the dialogue between the different characters. The mouse varies between being very demanding and rather whining. The other characters vary between crossness and being a bit more sympathetic.*
- *Props can make this story come to life. Find a little wooden or tin box that can contain some things you can use in the course of the story. Put in the box a small toy mouse (the kind you get in a pet shop is fine) and a selection of the things that the hat-maker might use for sewing (needles, thread, etc.). Then prepare two similar little hats, one plain, one decorated with sequins or braid. Put these, too, inside your sewing box, together with one or two small pieces of the material from which you have made the hats. The items can be brought out at appropriate times - mouse first, then a piece of material, next the plain hat and finally the decorated hat.*
- *The mouse's song can be as simple as you like. Hold your toy mouse in front of you, moving her along through the air as you sing the song. Encourage everyone to join in the singing.*

Follow-up activities

1. *Invite the children to draw pictures of the story.*
2. *Let the children make maps of the mouse's journey. Draw onto some sheets of paper simple winding roads onto which the children can add pictures of the shops and the palace.*
3. *Do craft work based on the story. Set up tables with materials for making mouse figures (e.g. corks for the body, card for the ears and nose, coloured wool for tails, etc.). Also set out materials for making hats for the mouse; for example, pieces of cloth, glue and sequins or braid.*

'The Little Red Monkey'

(retold from the picture book 'Little Red Monkey' by John Astrop)

Story summary

A naughty monkey plays tricks on the creatures of the jungle. They get fed up and decide to teach him a lesson. They trap him in a hole in the jungle and keep him there until he realises why and promises to be better in future.

Full version

Once in the jungle there lived a little red monkey who was always playing tricks. One day, he went to see the hippopotamus. The hippopotamus was wallowing in the mud at the time, but when he came out of the mud, the little red monkey painted pink spots on his back. The hippopotamus roared: "Who painted these spots on my back?"

And who was it? The little red monkey.

Another day, the little red monkey went to see the parrot. He saw the parrot's long tail of coloured feathers and pulled it. Yank!

The parrot squawked, "Who's pulling my tail?"

And who was it? The little red monkey.

Another day, the little red monkey went to visit the birds' nest. When the birds flew off to find some food, he put sharp prickly thorns in their nest. "Ouch!" said the birds when they came back. "Who's put these sharp prickly thorns in our nest?"

And who was it? The little red monkey.

The same thing happened with the little animals. He woke them with his drums when they were taking their afternoon sleep. And he tied the elephant's trunk in a knot, with the result that the elephant could hardly speak: "Who died my drunk in a dot?"

Finally the animals got so fed up, they decided to teach the little red monkey a lesson. They called a meeting and asked the elephant what they should do. The elephant thought about it (after they'd untied the knot in his trunk) and came up with a plan. "What do little red monkeys like to eat?" he asked.

"Bananas," the animals replied.

The elephant suggested they dig a hole in the jungle and fill it with bananas. When the little red monkey came along, he would start eating the bananas and, without realising what was happening, he would sink down into the hole. Then they would have him trapped in one place for once and they could tell him why they were angry.

Cooking Up a Story

That's what the animals did. They dug a hole, filled it with bananas and waited. When the little red monkey came along, he started eating the bananas and by the time he'd finished, he'd sunk down to the bottom of the hole. When he realised where he was, the little red monkey was frightened. "Get me out!" he shouted.

The animals came and looked down the hole. They reminded the little red monkey of all the tricks he had played. "Do you remember what you painted on my back?" said the hippopotamus. "Do you remember what you did to my tail?" asked the parrot. "Do you remember what you put in our nest?" said the birds. "Do you remember how you woke us up?" said the little animals. "Do you remember what you did to my trunk?" said the elephant.

"But I'll be good from now on," said the little red monkey. "Please get me out of the hole."

So they did. The elephant put down his trunk and lifted the red monkey out. Then the little red monkey did all kinds of things to make up for the naughty things he had done. Everyone was very happy.

Hints on telling

* *Introducing a song, The Little Red Monkey's Song, is an effective way to get and keep attention, and to link the episodes of this story:*
    > *la la la la*
    > *la la la la*
    > *what shall I do today I wonder?*
  Tap your knees in rhythm with the first two lines, rub your hands together gleefully during the third.
* *Find some way to bring each of the tricks to life with sound and action. Pretend to paint spots on the hippo's back, pull the parrot's tail (Yank!), show the birds flying away from the nest, bang the drums, etc.*
* *Encourage the children to participate in the story by joining in with your actions and sounds.*
* *When it comes to eating the bananas, pretend to unpeel them and eat them and take your time so that the children can get the idea. Count the bananas. Let the children join in.*
* *Invite children to contribute and discuss their own ideas. When the animals have their meeting to talk about what to do with the little red monkey, the children can say what they think. Some will probably say, "Kill him!" or "Get the police." Don't shout them down. Just discuss the pros and cons of their ideas with them. When the animals have to think about getting the monkey out of the hole, ask the children how this can be done. They will probably come up with lots of different plans.*

Follow-up activities

1. *This is a particularly good story for encouraging children to make their own pictures. Invite them to choose their favourite moment in the story as the basis of their picture.*
2. *Talk to children about their pictures. Inscribe what they say onto the bottom of their pictures.*
3. *Collect the pictures together into a book. Children will love to look at their book.*

'Two Birds in a Beard' – an adaptation of a folk-story from Thailand

Story summary

Two birds live in an old man's beard. One day, after the birds' five eggs have hatched, the father bird goes out searching for worms to feed the young ones and becomes trapped overnight inside a flower. When he returns next day, he is received very crossly by the female bird and a noisy argument begins. Then the voice of the old man tells the birds that they'll have to go and live somewhere else.

Full version

Far, far away there was a cave. Behind the cave was a dark, dark forest. Behind the forest were high, high mountains. Behind the mountains was a blue, blue lake. And on the lake grew big white flowers.

In the cave lived an old man who had a long, long, beard. And in the old man's beard there was a nest. And in the nest there lived two birds, Mr Bird and Mrs Bird.

One summer, Mr Bird and Mrs Bird had five eggs in the nest. They took it in turns to sit on the eggs until, one day, the eggs began to hatch. Soon there were five little birds, all of them calling for food.

Breakfast, breakfast, breakfast, breakfast, breakfast. Lunch, lunch, lunch, lunch, lunch. Tea, tea, tea, tea, tea. Supper, supper, supper, supper, supper.

Father Bird and Mother Bird had a busy time trying to keep their chicks well fed. From morn to night, they took it in turns to go out hunting for insects and worms. But one day, when Father Bird was out searching for food, he had nothing but bad luck. Wherever he looked, he could find no food.

He flew up from the cave into the tall dark trees. Nothing. He flew up over the trees to the high, high mountains. Nothing. He flew over the mountains to the big, blue lake. Nothing.

By the time he came to the lovely white flowers, he was extremely tired. Father Bird flew down to the flowers and came to rest in the centre of the biggest, whitest bloom. And there, at once, he fell fast asleep.

Unfortunately, while he was sleeping, the sun began going down in the sky. And as it went down, the big white flowers began to close their petals. Soon, the biggest flower was tightly shut with Father Bird inside.

When Father Bird woke up from his nap, he couldn't get out of the flower. He couldn't fly upwards without bumping his head. He couldn't fully open his wings. He realised he was trapped. But however loudly he called for help, there was no-one to hear him and no-one to come to the rescue.

Meantime, back in the nest, Mother Bird was waiting for Father Bird to return. Sometimes she felt anxious about him. Sometimes she felt cross and all round her, the little birds were cheeping.

This went on all night until at last the sun came up in the sky. And of course, as the sun began to rise over the big blue lake, the lovely white flowers began to open. First, Father Bird saw a crack of light. Then as the crack got bigger and bigger, he discovered he could open his wings. Joyfully, he flew up into the sky and headed home for the nest.

When Father Bird arrived, Mother Bird was waiting for him. "WHERE HAVE YOU BEEN?" she asked.

Father Bird replied. "I've been so worried about you. All night long, I was trapped in a flower."

"Trapped in a flower?" said Mother Bird crossly. "Do you expect me to believe that?"

And with that the two birds began to argue. As they argued, their voices got louder and louder. And the little chicks got hungrier and hungrier and began making more and more noise.

Suddenly, they all heard a strange new sound. It was a big, deep voice and it said, "YOU TWO BIRDS ARE MAKING TOO MUCH NOISE. YOU'LL HAVE TO GO AND LIVE SOMEWHERE ELSE!"

Do you know who it was? It was the old man. And that's when Father Bird and Mother Bird had to start looking for another place to make a nest. Luckily, by the time they had found a place they liked, the little birds were learning to fly.

And where do you think they made their new home? On a branch in one of the tall, dark trees. That's how birds started living in trees. They've been making their nests there ever since.

Hints on telling

- *This story allows for a great variety of hand gestures. You can set the scene by using gestures to conjure up the big cave, the trees, the mountains, the flowers and the old man's long beard. Cross your hands at the wrist and move them gently to suggest the birds flying around. A sense of drama enters the story when the birds' eggs begin to hatch. Cup your hands into an egg shape, then move them quickly to suggest the eggs hatching. Do the same thing five times and your listeners will start joining in. For the flowers, have your hands cupped together. Show your fingers opening out as the flowers open, coming together as the flowers close.*
- *The story also allows for variety of tone and expression. Emphasise the repetitiveness of the little birds calling for food. This is also a place where children can join in. Play-act Father Bird's distress when he finds he is trapped. Also play-act Mother Bird's different feelings when Father Bird doesn't come home. But be careful to judge how much emotion to use according to the children in your group. For some children, this could be a worrying scene. It is best to keep things light-*

hearted and as humorous as you can. It's a big surprise in the story when the old man speaks out at the end. Use a deep low voice. The children will probably guess who is speaking.

- Invite children to contribute their ideas to the story. Ask children at the end where the birds might choose to go and live. You could discuss the advantages of different places before saying that actually they went to live in the trees.

Follow-up activities

1. This is a good story for children to act out. You can allocate parts: an old man, Father Bird and Mother Bird, five little children to be the eggs that hatch into chicks.
2. The old man's beard can be a wonderful prop to make perhaps using long curls of white paper.

Cooking Up a Story

'The Magic Cooking Pot' – a traditional English tale

Story summary

A little girl is given a magic cooking pot which makes plentiful amounts of porridge for her and her mother. One day when the girl is not at home, the mother asks the pot to make more porridge but doesn't know how to stop it. The porridge overflows until the girl comes home and stops the pot by saying the right words.

Full version

Once there was a little girl who lived with her mother. They were very, very poor. One day there was no food to eat. So the mother sent her daughter out to the forest to collect some berries for their supper.

On the way, the little girl met an old woman. The old woman noticed that the girl looked very hungry.

"Yes," said the little girl, "I am very hungry."

The old woman said she could help. She got out a little cooking pot and gave it to the girl. She told her how to work it. She said that the little girl must always say this little rhyme to make the pot start:

> Hiss and bubble, little cooking pot.
> Make some porridge and make it hot.

When the pot had made enough porridge, the little girl must stop it working by saying another little rhyme.

The little girl took the pot home and told her mother all about it. Then she said the rhyme to make it start working. The little pot started hissing and bubbling and lots of porridge came up inside it. Soon there was plenty of porridge for supper and the little girl told the pot to stop:

> Thank you, little cooking pot.
> Now it's time for you to stop.

The porridge was delicious and the little girl and her mother were very happy. For the first time for a long time, they had enough to eat!

Every day after that, the little girl would get out her pot and make food for her and her mother. But one day when the little girl was out playing, the mother got out the pot and told it to make some porridge:

> Hiss and bubble, little cooking pot.
> Make some porridge and make it hot.

The pot started hissing and bubbling and lots of porridge came up inside it. When the pot was full, the mother tried to stop it. But she didn't use the right words. What she said was, "That's enough, little cooking pot."

And those weren't the right words to use!

Cooking Up a Story   35

So the pot carried on hissing and bubbling and more and more porridge came up inside it. Soon porridge was pouring over the sides of the table. It was flowing out of the kitchen door. It was covering the garden. It was everywhere!

Luckily after a while, the little girl came home. When she saw all the porridge everywhere, she rushed into her house and said the right words to the pot:

> Thank you, little cooking pot.
> Now it's time for you to stop.

Then the pot stopped making porridge and there was a lot of clearing up to do!

After that, it was only the little girl who used the pot. She always remembered the exact words to use and she and her mother always had just the right amount to eat.

Hints on telling

Preparing the children is half the battle. It will help them get ready for the magic.

- *You could start the session with Magic Pot, the imagination game on page 11.*
- *Or get out a little pot, a pretend one or a real one, and talk about rhymes that might encourage it to work some magic. You could make up a rhyme together.*
- *Or you could go on to say that you've got a story about a magic pot that made porridge and introduce the rhyme from the story:*
  > *Hiss and bubble, little pot*
  > *Make some porridge, and make it hot!*

Now you are ready to tell the story!

Cooking Up a Story

'The Yellow Blob' – a colourful story

Story summary

The Yellow Blob lives in a yellow world. One day he comes across a blue lake. After swimming in the lake, he discovers he is no longer yellow. He's what you get when you mix yellow and blue: green.

Full version

The Yellow Blob lived in a yellow world where everything was yellow. Yellow trees. Yellow grass. Yellow flowers…

Wherever you looked, it was all yellow. Yellow house. Yellow windows. Yellow door… When the Yellow Blob painted his hall, he didn't worry about which colour. He chose yellow. Primrose yellow. When he bought carpet for his stairs, the same thing happened. He got yellow. Sunshine yellow. And his bedroom was yellow too. Yellow bed. Yellow duvet. Yellow pillow…

One day the Yellow Blob woke up in the morning and his room was filled with yellow sunshine. He knew it was a day for an adventure. So he jumped out of bed. BLUMP!

He bounced down the stairs. BOUNCETY… BOUNCETY… BOUNCETY…

"I must have something to eat," he said and went into his yellow kitchen. There on the table was just what he fancied. Yes, it was a banana. So he peeled the banana and ate it up. But he still felt hungry. So he looked in the fridge and saw some yellow custard. YUM! It was delicious! And when he'd finished the custard, he went on his way. He went out of the door and down the road. CHICK-A-BOOM… CHICK-A-BOOM…

Soon he came to the yellow moor where all the tussocks of grass were yellow. BOUNCETY… BOUNCETY… BOUNCETY…

Further and further he went, and higher and higher. Until… BUMPETY BUMP! The Yellow Blob had met a hill. The Yellow Blob looked up at the hill. It was high, VERY HIGH. "That's not going to put me off," he said. "I'll climb that hill, I will, I will." So the Yellow Blob started to climb. ERCH… ERCH… ERCH…

PHEW!… He felt hot. After stopping for a minute, he started again… ERCH… ERCH… until he got to the top. "Hooray," said the Yellow Blob. "I did it." But when the Yellow Blob saw what was on the other side of the hill, he gasped. WOW!

On the other side of the hill was a big blue lake. The lake looked up. The Yellow Blob looked down. The water was blue and it looked very inviting.

Then the lake began to sing:

> Come on down, Yellow Blob.
> Come down here for a swim.
> It's lovely, it's cool.
> If you wait, you're a fool.
>
> Come on down, Yellow Blob,
> Come on down.

The Yellow Blob said, "I think I will."

So he stretched on his toes… one…. two…. three…. and he jumped. Down into the cool blue water. SPLASH! First he swam under the water… SWISH… Then… SWISH… SWISH… he swam to the side. SWISH… he pulled himself out.

And when he looked at himself, he had a big surprise. The Yellow Blob saw he had changed. He wasn't the Yellow Blob any more. He was what you get when you mix yellow and blue. He was GREEN.

So that's the story of how the Yellow Blob became the Green Blob. And next time you think of a story, maybe it'll be the story of the Green Blob and all the things that he did.

Hints on telling

- *You can tell this story with some paper and paint to demonstrate what happens when you put blue paint on yellow. You will need an easel with a white piece of paper plus pots of yellow, blue and green paint.*
- *Paint a large spot of yellow to show the Yellow Blob. Then paint a large patch of blue to represent the lake. Then paint a large spot of yellow onto the blue when the Yellow Blob jumps into the lake. Show how that patch of colour goes green.*
- *While you are telling the story, encourage the children to imitate and join in with all the actions: bouncing, eating, climbing, swimming.*

Follow-up activities

Give the children a chance to try out the magic of colours themselves with supplies of yellow and blue paint.

Variations

1. *Depending on how far you want to take the story, you can try making up other adventures for the Yellow Blob, or the Green Blob.*
2. *Or you can just discuss some ideas briefly with the children and go on to tell other colour stories. What about 'The Blue Balloon'? Or 'The Little Red Monkey' on page 30?*

'Andy the Ant Gets Angry' – a "feelings" story

Story summary

Andy the Ant and his family have made a new garden. Andy gets very angry when an elephant blunders towards it because it looks as if the elephant will destroy it. Andy tries to get him to go away and is extremely happy when he succeeds.

Full version

This is going to be an ANGRY story. It's going to be about an ant, an ant called Andy. Andy the Ant woke up one day and this is what I heard him say:

> I don't know what will happen to me today,
> I don't know how I'll feel,
> BUT... I'm going OUT!

It was early in the morning. Andy the Ant was very excited. He wanted to walk round his new garden. Andy's family was enormous: brothers, sisters, aunties, uncles, cousins, grandparents, mothers, fathers. They all lived together in the same little house and, in the last few weeks, Andy had been helping make a special new garden to give them a bit more space to relax in. Only yesterday, Andy had helped finish the garden with a fine new garden gate.

"Today," Andy thought, "the first thing I'll do is walk round the new garden to see if I like it."

He went straight outside. But what was that? What was that terrible noise? Something... somebody... was coming along... along the path towards Andy's new garden.

It was...

> something... somebody... with very big feet
> something... somebody... with very big legs
> something... somebody... with a very big body
> something... somebody... with a very big head
> something... somebody... with very big ears
> something... somebody... with a very big trunk

It was an ELEPHANT!

Boom... went the elephant's feet. Boom... boom...

The elephant was getting closer. Soon he would be stepping on Andy's new garden.

Suddenly Andy felt angry. He didn't feel frightened. He just felt angry. All that work, that lovely new garden. The elephant would smash it. He would ruin it all. Without delay, Andy peered through the gate and shouted.

"Go away, Elephant! Go back! Go away!"

But Elephant didn't hear. He just kept coming closer.

Boom... went the elephant's feet. Boom... Boom...

Cooking Up a Story

Andy shouted again. "Go away, Elephant, can't you hear me? You're not looking where you're going. Go away."

But Elephant didn't take any notice. He just kept coming closer.

Boom... went the elephant's feet. Boom... Boom...

By now Andy was very angry. Very, very angry indeed. Once again he shouted, and this time he did it so loudly he thought he was going to pop.

"STOP, ELEPHANT! LOOK WHERE YOU'RE GOING. GO AWAY!"

Suddenly Elephant stopped. "What's that squeaking?" he said in a deep rumbling voice that almost deafened Andy. "Who's there? What do you want?"

"It's ME," Andy answered. "Andy the Ant. I'm down here by the garden gate. You're coming too close to our garden. You're going to step on it. Please go away."

"Oh sorry," Elephant replied, looking down at Andy. "I didn't mean to upset you. I didn't plan on hurting your garden. I didn't even know you'd been making a garden. I'll go the other way."

And before you could say Hip Hip Hooray, Elephant turned in his tracks and went lumbering off in another direction.

"Phew!" said Andy. "That was a close one." And he went back into the house. He wasn't a bit angry any more. He just felt glad, and very relieved.

Inside the house, Andy's mother was getting things ready for breakfast. Andy told her what had happened.

"Well done, Andy," said his mother. "Sometimes it's worth getting angry." Then she gave him a hug and a nice cup of tea and Andy felt happy, and very, very proud.

Hints on telling

- *This is a story about one of the most common of all emotions: anger. It is important to communicate the emotion by the expression on your face and in your voice, but never in a way that might frighten your listeners.*
- *Use a big deep rhythmical voice to suggest the elephant's footsteps.*
- *Look up when you're taking the part of Andy, down when you're talking in the voice of the elephant.*
- *Make the ending sound very reassuring and happy.*

Making up other similar stories

- *You can follow a basic pattern if you want to make up new stories along similar lines. First choose a feeling. Then choose a creature who will experience the feeling. Next choose a name for the creature. An alphabetical match between the feeling, the creature and the name is a good idea: it gives rhythm to the story. Thus the angry story has an ant called Andy, while the frightening story on page 42 has a fish called Fatima. A happy story could have a hippo called Humphrey.*
- *The structure of the stories follows a pattern too. First the character in the story goes out. Then something happens which results in the character experiencing the emotion or feeling concerned. There are usually one or two obstacles to overcome. Then the story always ends on a happy note with the character coming back home to hugs and kisses and nice things to eat.*

'Fatima the Fish Gets a Fright' – another feelings story

Story summary

Fatima the Fish goes out to meet her new friends. On the way she sees a shark. She gets frightened but manages to get home safely. She tells the story of what happened and her new friends come to find her.

Full version

This is going to be a frightening story – and it's going to be about a fish. I wonder what the fish could be called? Something beginning with "f"? Fatima?

Fatima the Fish woke up one day, and this is what I heard her say:

> I don't know what will happen to me today.
> I don't know how I'll feel.
> BUT...
>   ...I'm going OUT.

Fatima the Fish was looking forward to seeing her new friends. She'd met them once when she swam to the other side of her usual rocks. Now she was hoping to see them again. So Fatima the Fish said all her goodbyes. "Goodbye," she said to her mother. "Goodbye!" she said to her father. "See you later." (You can add other goodbyes to her brothers and sisters).

Then Fatima went swimming out of her cave.

Fatima the Fish swam straight for the rocks. She knew the rocks very well. She knew all the short cuts for getting between them and all the hiding places where you could play peek-a-boo. But today Fatima swam straight past the rocks and on past the seaweed forest. She'd seen the seaweed forest a few times before. She knew it was big and you could easily get lost there. Today she didn't want to get lost. She wanted to find her new friends.

Fatima the Fish went swimming on. "Not far now," she thought. But soon after passing the seaweed forest, Fatima thought she saw a big open mouth.

"It's a shark!" she said. "It must be a shark!" And it seemed to be coming straight towards her. "Oh no!" said Fatima the Fish to herself. "I must get out of the way or it might eat me!"

So Fatima the Fish turned round very quickly. Before a second had passed, she was swimming for home as fast as her fins could take her.

Fatima was feeling frightened. She was sure the shark was chasing her. She was sure the shark was right behind her. Actually, it wasn't! It wasn't coming after her! It hadn't even seen her! But Fatima didn't know that.

Quickly, Fatima swam past the seaweed forest. Quickly, she swam for the rocks near her home. She thought, "If I can get to the rocks, I'll hide in one of my hiding places. Then I will be safe." So Fatima went on swimming until she got to the rocks. Quickly, she swam into one of the tiniest cracks. There she hid until she dared to peer out.

When Fatima looked out of her hiding place, she couldn't see an open mouth. She couldn't see a shark at all. She peered a little further out. She thought the shark had probably gone. But Fatima knew she must still be careful. So as she swam out from her hiding place, she looked all round her, again and again. But the shark was nowhere to be seen.

So Fatima the Fish went swimming home. When she came to her cave, she felt quite wobbly. But she was very relieved. She'd managed to get home safe. She told her family all about what had happened.

"Clever Fatima," said her mother. "Clever Fatima for swimming so fast. Clever Fatima for hiding in the rocks. None of us like sharks, they're much too big and hungry. So well done, Fatima, for getting out of the way." Fatima's mother gave her a nice fishy hug. Fatima's father gave her a fishy hug too and so did all her brothers and sisters. Now Fatima felt much, much better.

Then something even nicer happened. Fatima was just about to have a snack when she heard cheerful voices outside her cave. It was her new friends.

"Hello Fatima," said the fishes. "We didn't see you so we've come to find you. Do you want to come out to play?"

Fatima was pleased and excited to see her new friends again. She told them her frightening story, how she'd been coming to look for them when she saw a shark. Her new friends said, "That's funny. We don't usually see sharks in this part of the ocean. Maybe it was a shark who was lost! Perhaps he was trying to find his way home! Anyway, let's go out and play peek-a-boo in the rocks. And your brothers and sisters can come too."

So that's what they did. They had a wonderful time. And, funnily enough, after that frightening day, Fatima the Fish never saw a shark again.

Hints on telling

- *How to deal with emotion is as important in this story as in the previous tale of Andy the Ant. The story deals with fear in an especially direct and potent form - the fear of getting lost and being frightened by a stranger. It is important not to ignore these emotions. We all experience them. But it must not be done in a scary way. The idea is not to frighten the children but to allow them to recognise and work through something they may already have felt in their lives.*
- *The best technique is probably to keep close to the story while encouraging the children to predict what is going to happen and enabling them to participate in the usual actions and sounds.*

Follow-up activities

1. *Drawing different "feelings" faces onto paper plates makes a good preparation for these sorts of stories.*
2. *Making a mobile for each story would be a good follow-up, too. The mobile can combine the relevant alphabet letter with cut-out pictures that illustrate the story.*

Dessert

Notes on the sources of the action chants and stories

Mrs Wiggle and Mrs Waggle

This is one of many versions of an action story that has been kept alive by storytellers working in the oral tradition. Every storyteller's version differs slightly, or sometimes a lot, from every other storyteller's version. The story is often told with male characters, Mr Wiggle and Mr Waggle.

Going on a Bear Hunt

Michael Rosen's version of this traditional rhyme is available as a Big Book (Walker Books, 1997). Many variants of the rhyme can be found in America and elsewhere.

The Fly Called "Eee"

This highly participative story is an adaptation of a folktale which was told to me by a refugee mother from Sri Lanka who came to a storytelling course I was running. I gratefully acknowledge her original story which I have adjusted in various ways over many times of telling, including making the story into a rap.

Sun Frog and Moon Frog

This story was originally developed by the late Penny Bernand for a Pop-Up Theatre production. Based on the West African folktale of how the sun and moon got into the sky, it has been further embellished by myself in the course of many retellings and has proved immensely popular with young children.

Rabbit's Lucky Escape

Another debt of gratitude is owed to the person who told me this story at a storytelling workshop some time ago. Her background was Asian, though she grew up in East Africa, and she said she had often heard it told in her family when she was growing up.

The Naughty Little Mouse

This story, too, was passed on to me at a workshop. Told at the workshop by an Indian woman, it is one I have retold many times, always with great thanks to the person who passed it on to me and with pleasure in the children's response.

The Little Red Monkey

This story is closely based on the picture book by John Astrop, 'Little Red Monkey' (Hutchinson, 1977). Retold here in my own words, the story became one of the first that I consciously 'told' to children. This happened one day when I made up a theme song for the little red monkey and realised that I knew the picture-book so well, I could bring the story to life without the book.

Two Birds in a Beard

This story was told to me in a workshop by a woman from Thailand, who recalled it as being part of a longer story which she had heard as a child. It seems to me to provide a very complete experience as it is.

Magic Cooking Pot

This well-known folktale has been retold in many printed versions. There are many similar tales of magic kettles and so on in countries across the world.

The Yellow Blob

This story popped into my head, whole and complete, one day while I was walking in the park. It has proved popular with children right across the Primary age-range.

Andy the Ant Gets Angry

This story became the first of a long series of stories which I started making up when a nursery school asked me for some stories about "feelings". I discovered that the stories I created worked especially well if I consulted the children on what feeling they would like to have a story about, then let them choose a name for the main character. With my help, they chose names which shared the same first letter with the selected feeling. I also encouraged the children to do a lot of guessing and predicting about what was going to happen next in the story.

Fatima the Fish Gets a Fright

This story became another in the series of feelings stories. I discovered that this kind of story worked particularly well with ethnically mixed groups of children. In choosing names from those the children knew, it was possible to introduce a wide variety of names that do not generally appear in the published stories that are usually available to nurseries and early years classes.

Remembering a story

You may want to tell a story you've heard being told by someone else. Go through it in your mind, making it suit with your way of thinking and your personal style.

Or you may want to tell a story you've found in a book. Don't try to memorise it word for word. Instead, read it through a few times, then check if you remember the main points by skimming through it in your mind, noting down the key events or telling it silently to yourself.

Making the story feel like your own

Draw a series of pictures that illustrate your story or make a map of the locations. This will help you to feel that you have placed the story in your own mind.

Allow the characters in the story to talk to each other in your head. Listen to what they say and how they are saying it. This will give you ideas to add in to your telling.

Try closing your eyes and allowing your mind to dwell on some of the scenes in the story. You will probably find yourself visualising the story in great detail - setting, colours, emotions, etc. You can then select the details you want for your telling.

Introducing your story

It's a good idea to think about how you want to introduce your story. Picture books have covers and titles. A told story has to be introduced some other way. You might show an object that is related to the story. Or mention something interesting that is going to happen in it. Or just say you've got a story to tell.

Traditional beginnings (and endings)

Oral tradition offers many traditional beginnings (and endings) which help children get used to listening to stories. "Once upon a time..." is the familiar start, but you could try something else:

> A long, long time ago
> when little birds nested in old men's beards...

Or:

> Chin, chin, chin, my story's in.
> (In this case, the ending is Chin, chin, snout, my story's out.)

An unusual start could be:

> Once upon a time when pigs spoke in rhyme
> And monkeys chewed tobacco
> And hens took snuff to make themselves tough
> And ducks said, "quack, quack, quacko!"

Cooking Up a Story

A good ending is provided by:

> Snip, snap, snout
> My story's told out.
> And that's the end of it.

Preparing for participation

Think through places in the story where you can introduce:

> *Gestures and actions (a bird flying, a man climbing, an elephant walking)*
> *Sound effects (an owl hooting, a tap dripping, thunder roaring)*
> *Dialogue (two people talking to each other, two animals making sounds at each other)*
> *Rhythms or rhymes (tap your knee for a walking sequence; make up a little rhyme that can be repeated in the story)*

Children will usually need no encouragement to join in with the above, especially if you smile encouragingly at your audience!

Getting together your props

It is very helpful to find a couple of objects, perhaps a key, a fish, a comb, a hat, that will make your story visually attractive and help the children to understand what it's about.

Some people like to use puppets. But props do not have to be complicated to be successful. It's often best to have just a few.

Puppets or soft toys can also provide the basis for stories that you make up. Your stories might reflect recent events that have happened at nursery.

Discipline

Children love stories, and behaviour shouldn't be a problem if there are plenty of opportunities for them to join in. Rhymes, actions, sounds and gestures will capture their interest and attention, so it's unlikely that you'll need to stop them fidgeting and talking.

If you have children who are anxious or unsettled, try moving them nearer to you and helping them to join in. Even better is when there are other adults available to support your storytime. They can then sit with particular children who need help and encouragement.

A child who remains unhappy may need to leave the storytime until he or she is ready to come back. Storytime should be treated as a pleasure which it is a pity to miss.

Organising your storytime

It is worth bringing your storytime forward in your session, if not every time then at least once a week. This gives children an opportunity to "play" with the story after it has been told by drawing pictures, handling props, role playing the characters and events.

It is often preferable to have storytime somewhere other than in the book corner. There may be more room in another area, and you may feel freer to tell a story without using a book.

Seating the children in a wide semicircle, in two rows if necessary, allows you to feel near to them and ensures that they all have a good view of you.

By the end of the year, the older children should easily be able to manage (and enjoy) a storytime lasting 30 to 40 minutes. Younger children can often benefit from being with the older ones, especially if the storytime is lively and there is plenty of participation.

Special storytime groups

It can be very helpful to organise special small storytime groups for children who are shy and withdrawn or slow to speak. Small groups give children more adult attention and a better chance to be helped to participate, play story games, look closely at picture-books and so on.

Another idea with a lot of potential is to have a Storytelling Club which happens quite separately from the regular storytime. Taking place, say, once a week, a Storytelling Club can help raise the status of storytelling in your group and provide a welcome chance for staff to try out new stories or storytelling ideas.

Coffee & Mints

Some books about storytelling, story collections and other storytelling resources

Teresa Grainger, *Traditional Storytelling in the Primary Classroom*, Scholastic
A practical guide to storytelling with primary-age children and related classroom activities

Elizabeth Grugeon and Paul Gardner, *The Art of Storytelling for Teachers and Pupils*, David Fulton
A handbook on storytelling and how it relates to current literacy initiatives

Vivian Gussin Paley, *The Boy who would be a Helicopter, Storytelling in the Classroom*, Harvard University Press
An American teacher's account of working with a kindergarten class where stories are placed at the heart of the curriculum

Some collections of stories

Hugh Lupton, *The Story Tree: Tales to Read Loud*, Barefoot Books
A collection of stories with the emphasis on the oral

Mary Medlicott, *The Little Book of Storytelling*, Featherstone Education
A collection of stories and other material for telling to young children

Sophie Windham, *The Orchard Book of Nursery Stories*, Orchard Books
Simple straightforward tellings of well-known traditional tales for young children

Useful organisations

The following can provide details of storytelling events, directories of storytellers and information packs:

The Society for Storytelling
PO Box 2344
Reading RG6 7FG   Tel: 0118 935 1381

The Scottish Storytelling Centre
43-45 High Street
Edinburgh EH1 1SR   Tel: 0131 557 5724

The Verbal Arts Centre
Bishop Street
Derry
Northern Ireland BT48 6PU   Tel: 028 7126 6946.

Acknowledgements

Special thanks are due to the various people who told me the following stories at storytelling workshops and courses:

'The Fly Called "Eee"'
'Rabbit's Lucky Escape'
'The Naughty Little Mouse'
'Two Birds in a Beard'

Special thanks are also due to the late Penny Bernand of Pop-Up Theatre for her story, 'Sun Frog and Moon Frog'.

Also my grateful thanks to John Astrop for generously allowing me to retell in my own words his story, 'Little Red Monkey'.

Special gratitude goes to storyteller colleagues, especially Karen Tovell, who provided the inspiration and ideas for some of the rhymes and imagination games in this book.

Finally, I would like to acknowledge my indebtedness to Laura Borner and her colleagues in the London Borough of Enfield for enabling and encouraging me to produce the Storytelling Cookbook, from which this book has been developed.